ADVANCED PRAISE

"Penda is a gatherer, thought provoker, a seed planter, and a birther of dreams and visions implemented by God!"

~Danada Beckwith

This book is a reminder of the strength you carry. In life, you will face opposition, but never let your opposers determine how far you will go. Rather, be prepared to push yourself through every huddle until you get to the finish line— exactly where God wants you to be.

Until God says it's over, the sky is your limit.

~Sally Bossman, Author
The Relentless Woman

This rendition is an incredible smooth drink of tea with beautiful expressions of love and resilience. The moments in the heart of this book opened my mind, my eyes and heart. She remembered her strength. Oh! how prophetically named PENda, she is called to write!

Don't miss this opportunity to be present in your own life because you were created for more.

~Cheryl Denise Latimer, Executive Director
The Kingdom Direction

"*Remember Your Strength* is a captivating story of the beauty in resiliency. I appreciated Mrs. Penda's storytelling style and historical perspective. Your strength will truly be remembered and transformed!"

~Trizah O., Author
Falling in Love with Jesus: A 31 Day Devotional

"If you have ever found yourself struggling with your identity, purpose, beliefs, or convictions as a child of God, you want to read Remember Your Strength. Penda's authentic testimony of her back-and-forth relationship with God, emotional challenges of being judged and ridiculed by other Christians, and her road to rediscovering who God called her to be, is inspirational!

As a minister of the Gospel who is a life coach, this book reminded me of the importance of how we introduce others to Christ and subsequently walk alongside them on their faith journey until they find the strength, through Christ Jesus, to stand in their God-given purpose and destiny."

~Renita Quick, Co-Author
The Power of Agreement

"The year 2020 was a recalibration for resilience. Many did not make it out whole, and prayerfully, this book will bring them back into calibration."

~La Dina Strawder, Author
Love Wins: Nikki's Tale and Killing Grace: A Rise to Restoration

Also, By Penda L. James

Free to Fly: Wisdom for the Seasons in a Woman's Life
Girl, Pray for Me: Moving Toward Unpluckable Faith
Girl, Walk with Me: Unpluckable Faith and Accountability
Dandelion Dance
First, Lady: Selah
First, Lady: Called, Confident & Committed Woman in Leadership

REMEMBER Your Strength

Remember Your Strength: A Restorative Memoir

Copyright © 2024, by Penda L. James

ISBN: 978-1-7361824-8-2
Library of Congress Control Number: 2024903132

Published by: InSCRIBEd Inspiration, LLC.
Printed in the United States of America

Cover Photo: HD Visuals, Hannah Davis

Internal Layout and Design: InSCRIBEd Inspiration, LLC.

Cover Design: Bridgette Rooks www.cre8tivevibes.com, Penda L. James

Edited by: Charmaine Harris, Donna Harrison, Janese Jackson,
      Penda L. James, Nyota Robinson

All real-life anecdotes are told with permission from actual parties involved and recorded to the best of the author's recollection. Names in some instances have not been used at the request of the individuals referenced. In some cases, parties mentioned are deceased. Details of some instances have been slightly modified to enhance readability, or to ensure privacy. Any resemblance of any other parties is purely coincidental.

All rights reserved. No part of this book may be reproduced or transmitted in any form electronic, or mechanical, including photocopying and recording, or held in any information storage and retrieval system without permission in writing from the author and publisher.

NO AI TRAINING: Without in any way limiting the author's [and publisher's] exclusive rights under copyright, any use of this publication to "train" generative artificial intelligence (AI) technologies to generate text is expressly prohibited. The author reserves all rights to license uses of this work for generative AI training and development of machine learning language models.

DEDICATION

For my parents, **"Wonderful" Will and Marilyn Horton.** They modeled strength which allows me to stand unwavering in my own.

Remember Your Strength: A Restorative Memoir is for the strength in you, dear Reader, that often goes unrecognized because you need to inhale courage and exhale fear in order to remember it.

ACKNOWLEDGEMENTS

My gratitude runs deep. Special thanks to my **Unpluckable Faith Community** specific to this project:

- My siblings **Joi, JC,** and **Fred** – We are the Wonderful Legacy and create "Porches of Knowledge"
- **Angelique**, It had to be you to teach me how to surrender and coach me to finish.
- **Charmaine** believes in "Dr. Penda"
- **Diana** would not let me shrink
- **HD Visuals** captured me in pictures
- **Jai**, my Special soror, said, "Get it done"
- **Janese** edits with love and heart
- **La Dina** believed
- **Nneka** told me to give my best offering
- **Shea** told me the truth in love
- **Starr** took stunning photos and videos
- **Mariama** wrote a beautiful song
- **Sherrie** held me accountable
- **Nyota** edited and confirmed the gift
- **Bridgette Rooks** (Cre8tive Vibes) told me to, "Go be gre8t"
- This book would not have been possible without the people who shared their bounce-back stories with me.
- To the numerous friends and family I did not name, thank you for bringing me back home.

And, to **RJ** and **Amaris**, my love for you is my shield and sword.

CONTENTS

I Am Because We Are 3

A Wonderful Legacy 11

God Is. 21

Searching For God 37

Press Toward The Mark 53

Be Resolute 59

Stay In The Bubble 79

Stretch Out And Let Go 93

A Product Of Resilience 103

Conclusion–I Remember 111

References 117

FOREWORD

Have you ever left the house in a rush, grabbing everything you thought you needed? Keys: check, lunch: check, purse: check, coffee: checkity-check. You blaze out the house and into your day. You muddle through another workday and on the way home, you hear the dreaded sirens and see lights in your rearview.

"I just wanna get home. This day... UGH, THIS DAY," you mutter, frustrated, as you wait for the officer to leave their vehicle and hit you with the one-two punch... "License and registration please." One more deep sigh before they're at your window and business commences, as usual. Or almost as usual. You grab your registration from the glove box and reach inside your purse for your wallet...but there is no wallet. "Oh God; can this day get any worse?!"

Driving without a license. How many of us are guilty? Maybe you haven't been operating a motor vehicle without a valid license, but you've been walking around, existing each day, having forgotten your identification. Your ID. Who are you? Do you even remember? Did you ever really know? From experience, I can tell you that sometimes life hits so hard that it feels like it's knocked the truth out of you.

Knocked the wind out of you. Knocked the life out of you.

I guess that's what a TKO is. You're technically alive, but mostly unconscious. You go to work and back home, all on auto pilot. You wake up dreading each day because each day consists of enduring more of that abuse from family, from "friends," from bosses, from spouses. Your kids have conversations with a Madame Tussaud's wax figure of you while you stand over the stove making breakfast, lunch, and dinner.

They talk, but you don't hear words. They pour out to vacillating choruses of, "uh huh," "oh, that's nice," "Mmm." You go through the motions with your spouse because you have given too much and received too little and now, you're on your last drop of loving effort in the desolate, unforgiving, unrequited wilderness that is your marriage.

Maybe I haven't scratched the surface of your own personal amnesia-inducing experience; but whatever life has thrown at you, it's left you bloodied, bruised, eyes swollen shut from the relentless beating…well, this book is for you.

For you, whom life has brutalized so fully that you've started to forget who you are, what you're here for, and that you really matter, Penda, or "Lady P" as I call her, has compassionately penned this love letter to salve your wounds and Will you back to life; the pun is intended if you know her Dad's name. She wants to remind you of the stuff from whence you come and the fortitude that the sum of your life experiences has cultivated within you. This love letter is meant to stoke the fire that you carry inside. The one you thought had long since died. The one on which you'd given up hope.

Consider this love letter your personal Rafiki, a lá Lion King. It's come to help pull you out of the sunken place and may knock you upside the head a time or two to help you get the point. My earnest prayer is that by the time you get done reading, you are no longer lying face down on the mat awaiting the ref's standing eight-count, but you will start to come back to life. You will start to stir and pick yourself up and regain your clarity, your stability…your identity.

You see, because the hope that we find in my starting analogy is that while you may be in the car without your ID, you STILL HAVE ID, you just need to GET. BACK. HOME. And figure out where you left it. I love you, Friend.

Please don't give up on you.

Angelique Strothers, Author
In Pursuit of Surrender

PREFACE

"She is a friend of my mind. She gather me, man. The pieces I am, she gather them and give them back to me in all the right order."

~Toni Morrison, Beloved

I heard Pastor Keion Henderson say in one of his sermons, "What made me is what you never saw." Whew, there is so much truth to that for my life! There was a period of time that I believed in God, but my faith leaked out of me slowly like air in a tire, until I was completely flat. Walking with God required a power that I did not have.

I am writing *Remember Your Strength* as a woman who, after years of hiding, has finally recognized that she has a purpose that would not die, even when she tried to smother it.

From April 20, 2016, through March 13, 2023, I was in a fog. Events in my life knocked the wind out of me and I lost sight of myself. To cope, I buried myself in my roles of pastor's wife, mother and entrepreneur, but I struggled to find my faith. I didn't stand in the promises of God, nor did I even recognize how to reach out to Him for strength.

When I grew tired of fighting battles that do not belong to me, I surrendered the burdens of my heart to God in order to confront things that no longer served me. That is when I found my strength. When life hits you hard, you must remember your strength in order to rise again.

In this memoir, I talk about my pain, healing, and restoration openly— with no holds barred. You will learn how I responded to grief, disappointment, and rejection. I write honestly about putting on a cloak of the mythical "strong Black woman" and refusing to admit my indignation toward God when I was disappointed in His will for my life.

On the other side of my healing, I know that I was inconsistent in my faith. I either trusted Him out loud with words and no actions, leaned into my faith with full assurance that He would keep His promises, pouted when I didn't get my way, or pressed through difficult situations to get to my promise. Honoring my humanity, and the range of those reactions, I am grateful that I survived when I wanted to quit.

Throughout this book you will read about my healing journey. I not only share some of my poetry and prose, but there are declarations of strength from a few special people in my life. I interviewed them podcast style on what I called, "The Resilience

Project." This series of interviews that I hosted on social media brought pieces of me back home. From the bounce back stories of my guests that gave me strength to heal, albeit publicly, to the revelations God gave me, I learned that I could no longer hide in the background. I am too important.

My family emphasized the importance of reading and writing. I sat in the bed with my grandmothers and read books. My mother wrote affirmations and taped them to my mirror. My father taught me that when I write from my heart and someone else reads it, I have captivated their full attention. I believe that writing is one of the most important things we can do to ensure that our legacy remains. And my family nickname is "Pen," so I have a responsibility to this work.

There are several poems that I have penned when I needed clarity, and the rest of my memoirist reflections chronicle how I found my way back to faith, love, hope, and restoration. My biggest regret is that a major chunk of my teenaged and young adult years is not included. Remember Your Strength is important because I want us to curate our stories of resilience and hold them close. This is how we remember the tangible evidence of God's hand on our lives.

I will never forget sitting on the hardwood floor in my bedroom, ripping pages from the spine of a beautiful green and orange kente-cloth journal that my mother gave me. I was shredding the musings of my mind into confetti and discarding the tear-stained pages into the dumpster. At the time I did not know how to overcome the shame of my missteps and shortcomings. As a 19year-old college student, I could not imagine at the time, that my journal was a key to my healing.

As we take this journey, I want you to keep in mind a statement that my husband Robert spoke to me. He said, "When your faith returns to the source, throw off your cloak." When I threw off my cloak, I opened myself up to receive the pieces of me that were called home. Toni Morrison's words became true for me.

I wrote this restorative memoir to remind myself what strength means for the generations behind me. Yes, this is my story, but I want you to create your faith blueprint. I hope that my offering helps you remember your strength. Writing restored me and I want to help you recognize what made you who you are today.

Pick up the pen and let your heart speak,

Penda

> *"It is the family that is around you that helps you become the person that God created you to be."*

"Family Matters"
~Ronald A. George, Interview

I AM BECAUSE WE ARE

The PBS show "Finding Your Roots," hosted by Dr. Henry Louis Gates, Jr. follows Dr. Gates' team as they investigate the ancestry of a family. Influential people, including celebrities, request information about branches in their family tree and learn about ancestors they did not get the opportunity to meet.

The best part of the show for me, is the resolution of a family mystery. In honor of my love for the show, I am starting this book with my family history because my journey to restoring my strength started with remembering them, their sacrifices, and their resilience.

Tenacity =
the quality or fact of being very determined;
determination

I have no reason to question my tenacity. I come from chain breakers. I intentionally honor the fabric of my family, they are stitched into me, hand-sewn like the quilts I used to make with my

Grandma Horton. When my life's circumstances have worn me down, I may have felt defeat temporarily, but I believed that the word "quit" was not to be in my vocabulary. During those times it was necessary to revisit the strength I was born from. I can't lie to you, there have been times when I straddled the thin line of faith and doubt. Thankfully, I inherited a strength of my people that was forged by faith and fire.

Unfortunately, there is not much information recorded about the generations of Hortons (my dad's family) and Pitts (my mom's family) before me. The verbal history has stopped being passed down and the memories are not recorded. However, as I gathered what was accessible to me and reviewed it, I was fortified. Their stories reminded me that I am not designed to quit.

I know from my mother's journals and my father's oral history that my bloodline is traced to Blackfoot Indians and Africa. We have roots all over the world: the West Indies, Texas (Fort Hood, Dallas, Rosebud, and Houston); Salzburg, Austria; Lawton, Oklahoma; Alabama (Birmingham, Evergreen, and Uriah); Pensacola, Florida; Ohio (Toledo, Cleveland, Cincinnati, and Dayton); and Maryland (Baltimore and Cheverly).

In my family there were farmers, sharecroppers, educators, musicians, entrepreneurs, and community leaders. To that fact, my parents always made it clear to me that the life I cherish is the result of someone else's sacrifice. The same year I was born, my great grandfather ran for public office in Birmingham, Alabama. I don't know the outcome of the election.

My father made it mandatory for me and my siblings to learn about our history by reading books such as *Pimp* by Ice Burg Slim and *The Autobiography of Malcolm X*. As a family we often watched documentaries and attended events to hear about Black people who did great things. Every year we celebrated Kwanzaa and made handmade gifts to share with the community.

A highlight of every year for my family was watching the Lou Rawls Parade of Stars. Daddy used to say with pride, "All of my kids are going to attend an HBCU." Historically Black Colleges and Universities (HBCUs) are the pride and joy of our community. I cherish my experience at Wilberforce and some of my best memories were made in college. Yes, all four of Will and Marilyn's kids did attend an HBCU, and we all graduated from college. Only one of us graduated from a Predominately White Institution (PWI).

Generational Influencers

As the oldest child born to my parents, I had the opportunity to meet all my grandparents—all four were born between 1923 and 1930. They collectively experienced Jim Crow in the south. My grandparents lived through recessions and worked their way back into prosperity, leaving an inheritance for their children's children.

Listening to my grandparents talk, my imagination always used to run wild with crazy thoughts about their plight. I sometimes felt nervous when I was around people who didn't look like me, but my family always made sure we had intercultural connections that broke down racial barriers. Even though I have been able to sit anywhere I wanted to sit on any public bus, most times I went straight to the back which was a contradiction to Jim Crow on public transportation.

I have never worked in a chicken factory plucking feathers. When I was thirsty, I didn't have to drink from a segregated water fountain. Grandma Horton was asked, "How many bubbles are in a bar of soap?" when she registered to vote. As a voter, I never had to answer ridiculous questions, nor have I faced harassment at the voting polls.

Both my paternal and maternal grandfathers fought in World Wars. Grandpa Pitts won a Purple Heart for his bravery for rescuing his unit when their tank rolled over, even though he was injured. My mom's mother was named Hubert, but we called her Grandma Dear. Her soulful singing was marinated in southern love and grace which was passed down from her mother. Her melodic voice wrapped itself around you like a hug and rocked you into peace.

My mom told me about her grandmother, Octavia Rankin being lionhearted. She pulled her shotgun on the town sheriff after he ate at the café she owned and tried to leave without paying. That was a boss move from "Mama Tavie," a black woman in the

1930's. That action could have gotten her lynched. Unlike my grandparents and their parents, I have never picked cotton. My grandma, Elna Horton, told me about working the cotton fields in Barnesville, Georgia:

> *"Ain't no hard work ever killed nobody; it just made us better. We picked cotton on our own property. My grandfather had his own farm. After my uncle died, we moved in with Grandma because she couldn't work all that land too good by herself.*
>
> *I started helping when I was around eight years old. I didn't wear shoes, we went bare feeted; except in the winter when we had one pair of shoes. We picked cotton twice a year, once in the summer and the scrappy in October."*

As if I were a member of Dr. Gates' research team, I investigated the history of my family and uncovered gems of strength. My people were resilient because there was no other choice. My great uncle Marvin Howard, Grandma Horton's brother, used to say, "I'm feelin' fine, satisfied, and happy." Now I understand what he meant when he used to say that to me.

There is always a reason to live in gratitude and I stand on this firm foundation of strength.

WRITE Down

I told you all of this so that you can think about and find your own strength. Go follow the roots of your family tree and find the overcomers in your bloodline. You are one of them.

- How do you define family?
- What ideals do you hold onto when you feel forsaken?
- What are some interesting things that you know about your biological family? Or the family you have curated?
- List significant people in your bloodline and a few unique details about them.
- How has your family given you strength?

"Everyone wants to win; we are victorYOUs through our faith.
YOU are in the victory and that is by your faith."

"I Have VictorYOUs Faith"
~La Dina Anderson, Interview

A WONDERFUL LEGACY

My parents, Will and Marilyn Horton, loved music as much as they loved each other. Although they didn't lead solo selections in church, or march down the aisle wearing choir robes, there was always music playing, and somebody was usually singing in our house.

One of my dad's best friends, Uncle CB, informed me that he knew my mom and introduced her to my dad in college. The story is that people clamored over my mom because she was so beautiful with her fair skin, long hair, and slim figure. A lot of men were afraid to talk to her because Granddaddy Pitts was a principal, known for taking a paddle to many a student who got out of line in Toledo, Ohio.

I think my daddy probably was smitten with her immediately. His fraternity brothers called him "Wonderful." I can imagine that day, when he saw Marilyn, his eyes lit up and the word took on new meaning. They weren't in love at first sight, but love drew them to each other.

There was probably music and dancing at Uncle CB's house that day. My parents and their friends always had a good time, and their laughter was usually loud and boisterous. They were smokers, so cigarette smoke mixed with the scent of my mom's cooking probably enveloped the air. She was always cooking. They say she had the skills to make a six-course meal out of a can of beans and a box of cake mix.

I don't need to know all of the specific details, about how Wonderful and Marilyn got together. What is important to know is that on October 8, 1977, they were married in mom's hometown, Toledo, Ohio. My parents stayed married through the good and bad times of life well into forty memorable years.

Will plus Marilyn equals me, their oldest baby: Penda Lynn Horton. What can I say, God's timing is perfect, even if I was a surprise to them. I am Marilyn's daughter. Her fight for my life gave me the Will to live. I am Will's daughter, because I am wrapped in wonder, full of love, and such a cutie!

My Birth Song

At a writer's workshop a few months after my 30th birthday, I captured some of my unspoken birth history through a poem. The assignment was to announce to the world that I was coming. I sat still, closed my eyes, and let my pen guide me. I couldn't write fast enough, the words poured out of me and at one point I started to sing. By the time I finished, I was crying!

I was living in Colorado, and when I called my mom she said, "How did you know all of that?" I don't know how I knew some of the details that I captured with my pen, but this is what flowed out of me. I allowed my heart to pen my birth song, yet it was an accurate depiction of my arrival.

Penda's Birth Song (5/16/2004)

Sing.
Sing this song for Penda.
She is a bundle of love who embodies the name
her Daddy gave her.

He said, "This is my love child.
I want her words to blow people's minds.
She is coming at a time of war, but her presence brings peace.

She will be a canvas, open for expression."

Sing.
Sing this song.
Sing, for Penda.

Born unwanted and wanted in the March of 1974
Too soon, but just in time for change

Afros and bell bottoms
"Play that funky music white boy" for black girls like her at the party who dance with their daddies and step on their feet

Sing.
Sing this song.
Sing for Penda
Watch as she loves like her Mommy
She says, "They seek fortunes in cookies and love in the bed, but you sweet daughter Will be different.

You will know pain, you will thirst for healing and use it to quench others."
Sing this song.
This song, sing, for Penda and teach her to live.

Do you see the thread of music that flows through my birth song? Did you catch how I captured what my parents thought and said? I wrote about the Vietnam War, the fact that I was born premature and that I was an unexpected but welcomed child.

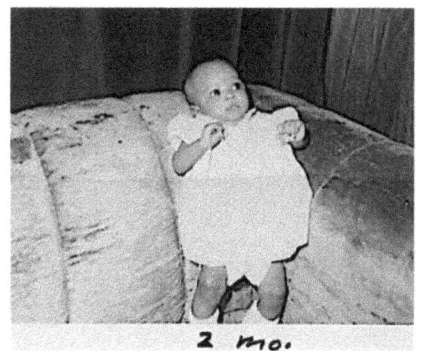
This picture was taken the same month that my great grandfather, Green Horton ran for office in Alabama in 1974.

There was a tug of war for my existence and my mom's fight for my life prevailed. My birth song reminded me of the intentionality behind my life. Sitting still with my pen that day, I guess I allowed my heart to speak, and it repeated what had been said about me.

Write your birth song and announce to the world who you are.

The Birth Order

I have one blood uncle. Other people call him "Marvelous" Marv, but I call him Uncle Marv. He is one of the most dedicated and loyal men I have ever met. He and I are 18 years apart, so it was fun when he was around. My mom has two sisters, Aunt Avie and Aunt Roz. Aunt Avie is living with the effects of a stroke/aneurism, but she is a pillar in my life. Aunt Roz is a diligent ministry leader and community servant. She carried the weight of caring for Grandma Dear in her later years.

I have three younger brothers and one younger sister. My younger brother, William Christopher Horton, III, died when I was five and he was five months old. I didn't really get a lot of time with him, but I do have significant memories of us. A five-year-old can't really verbalize how death impacts them, they just know that something is different. I remember feeling sad for a long time, and lonely after he died. This was an unspoken shift in our family, no one ever really talked about it. I think my brother's death was one of the first major tragedies that impacted my parents.

I recall my mother saying that she knew Christopher was dead because he was gray when she went to pick him up that morning. I was in kindergarten, and all I remember is that a neighbor took me home until it got dark. When mom picked me up and walked me home, my brother was not there. The eeriness of his crib being in our room made me restless. I kept thinking of him falling out of the bed the night before. The thought lingered with me that maybe if I had been a better big sister, he would not have died.

Thus, I became a fierce big sister when my siblings Joi, JC , and Fred were born. My parents taught me that I needed to protect them. I tried to cradle them like they were fragile eggs. To this day, I secretly worry about my siblings, even though we are all grown. If a situation arises and they are in need, I will lay my life down to protect them. Truthfully, now that our parents are gone, it's hard for me to step back from protecting them and stepping up as an elder at the same time. I still want to protect them from unnecessary breakage, but they have their own strength to lean on.

When Chris died in the Seventies, there were not a lot of prevention programs about Sudden Infant Death Syndrome (SIDS). No one really talked about the importance of placing a baby on their back to sleep or swaddling them for comfort. Bed bundles sold during that time had bumpers and comforters, which are no longer appropriate.

I don't know if blankets were a factor in Chris' death, but my sister, Joi and my brother, JC, had to wear a monitor when they were born two, and three years later. Experiencing death at such an early age, I think I was deflated by grief and did not know how to verbalize it to my parents.

Grandma Dear kept Christopher's memory with a ceramic figurine that she used to keep on display. When we visited, I would stand at the curio cabinet in her bedroom and think of him. Grandma Dear would always say, "That's my little angel baby." When she died and it was discarded, I was really heartbroken because I didn't think to ask anyone to save it for me.

- If you have siblings, what was it like growing up in your family?
- If you are an only child, were you close to anyone growing up?
- What does your family history teach you about yourself?

"Leaning on God is hanging on to the foundation and the trust that I can rebuild even when everything else seems to be devastated or gone. God is that solid foundation."

"I Lean on God;"
~Danielle Graham, Interview

GOD IS. . .

"My faith was built on love: serving a loving God, loving people, and living in God's transforming love."

My daddy was a deeply spiritual man. He had deep rooted faith that rested on one premise: "God Is All There Is!"

In his early years, my father was a Christian. He studied several religions throughout his life including Islam, Religious Science, and Daoism because he was searching for God. In his later years he shadowed life like it was a teacher, and he was the teacher's pet. At Teacher's instruction he watched his surroundings, studied people, and imitated things he thought would make him a better man. My father sat at the feet of great teachers, read books, and listened to recordings of some of the most revered spiritual leaders around the world. He did not ascribe to one religion; Daddy called himself a Gnostic. My father saw God in everything; he was the priest of our home.

Gnostic =

"possessing knowledge, especially esoteric knowledge of spiritual matters"

~www.Dictionary.com

In my family home at 202 N. Paul L. Dunbar St., a sign hung for a long time in our parlor. The declaration, accented in bright purple, red, and gold, in my father's handwriting, was a simple drawing of the phrase, "God Is All There Is!" The message was a flag that hung over us. It was a magnet of the God within us, drawing people who needed God, loved God, and wanted to talk about God. Although the sign is no longer hanging, its significance still guides me and my siblings.

If you don't know who he was, Paul Laurence Dunbar was one of the most prolific and celebrated Black writers in the late 1800s, early 1900s. Maya Angelou, my favorite writer, always credited him. Her book, I Know Why the Caged Bird Sings was inspired by his poem "Sympathy."

Mr. Dunbar's work highlighted the Black experience, and he was able to masterfully capture the voice, tone, and hope of our people. He was born to an escaped slave and a freed slave; a dark son yearning to be accepted as a man, but scorned at times because he was a Black man. And, I must add that he was briefly married to Alice Dunbar Nelson, a powerhouse of a writer and educator.

Many people in the community knew my mom because she worked at a local non-profit, in the food pantry. She would walk, or roller skate to work, keeping her connected to the people and always observing their needs, sometimes firsthand.

She was mindful as she would say, "not to shove a box in their faces." Mommy's greatest personal achievement was helping to design a Choice Food Pantry—a place where they could choose their own food. She wanted people to maintain their dignity, even in their time of need.

The Porch of Knowledge

No matter what time of year it was, you could find my daddy sitting on his front porch. There was always music playing and it would be loud! If you walked up, or drove by, in the rain, snow, sleet, or hail, if Daddy was on the porch he would turn the volume down to greet you, then crank it back up and snap his fingers or sing.

Daddy called himself "the Mayor of Paul Laurence Dunbar Street," and his house, on the corner of First and Paul Laurence Dunbar, was an anchor in the community. Across the street stands the Paul Laurence Dunbar State Memorial, the house he bought for his mother and lived in for the last three years of his life. Many people came to the "Porch of Knowledge" to sit at my daddy's feet and bop to his eclectic collection of tunes. There was funk, rock, jazz, rap, country, you name it. I used to laugh so hard when people would slow down to see if he was on the porch and then scream really loud, "Hey Will!" He would wave his hand and they'd speed down the street.

In a sense, my father was a gatekeeper, and he took that role seriously. He was a watchman on the wall. If he saw some unsavory activity on his property, or near it, he would stand up and exclaim, "Hey! We don't do that around here, take that sh-t on, and go somewhere else!" When Wonderful entered any room, you knew he was there. You either loved him or hated him. Either way, when you left his presence, his fingerprint was on you. My daddy's personality was big and sometimes misunderstood. He was big in personality, but one thing he always told us was, "Maintain your humility."

Paul Laurence Dunbar and Me

I grew up on Miami Chapel Road in Dayton, Ohio, but when my parents moved to Paul Laurence Dunbar Street, I was in high school. A 17-year-old, ready to be grown woman. I was getting ready to leave for college. My youngest brother, Fred was just a few months old. The summer of 1991, Dayton was a bustling city full of events and activities. Every summer we used to have community block parties and festivals that always had a parade. The Black Culture Festival was one of the highlights every summer in our city. When we moved to Dunbar Street, I saw life through different lenses.

Living in the corner house on the main thoroughfare of the parade route was exhilarating. I used to walk with friends to that side of town to see the parade, but living there, I had a front row seat to all of the action. We stood on the sidewalk and watched community organizations bounce down the street tossing candy at children and passing out flyers. The taps from drill team boots clacking against the brick street, colorful flags and dancing feet brought the community together.

The sound of the drums from the drum corps called to the community, luring us outside to commune and celebrate. For us, these parades were like being in New Orleans during Mardi Gras season. Those moments were like family reunions, they ignited my pride for Dayton, Ohio, "The Gem City." I loved living on Paul Laurence Dunbar Street. Our house was in walking distance to The Drew Health Center where people went for medical care or met for community meetups. That section of town was the hub of our community and the birthplace of my creative awakening as a scribe.

At the Dunbar House I sat at the feet of Laverne Sci, who curated stories and history for many years. As a family, we held events at the Dunbar House and volunteered our time to support her and the mission of the house. Like

Paul, we wanted to give back to our people. Going to the museum and hosting events there, I felt a responsibility to write with purpose. I wanted my words to be impactful, poignant and call people to action, like Paul's had done.

- Do you have a "porch of knowledge" to glean wisdom? How often do you sit there?
- Write about something you learned there or someone who has inspired you.

Is God. . .?

I recognize that I saw the world through compassionate eyes at an early age. My creative senses were heightened when we moved to Dunbar Street. I went to college at Wilberforce University on a mission to become a productive citizen.

As an adult, I can now say that I understand the call on my life to serve hurting people. Both of my parents were ambassadors for community; we are a family that lived, worked, and served people who came to us from all walks of life. It was and still is, a vital thread of who I am as a person.

I was always drawn to environments where broken, rejected, and neglected people would be. When I met my husband RJ we worked well together, serving people. RJ told me that he was called to be a pastor. For me to marry him, I had to carry a mantle of ministry, or I would have been miserable.

As a child I revered God and tried to stay humble in His presence by doing "good deeds." My daily goal was to be a good person. I had learned in my family church, The First Church of Religious Science, how to be a vessel for God and let His perfect love shine through me.

As I developed my love for God I willingly participated in my church's activities while in junior high and high school. I remember volunteering to serve food for homeless people, having connections with intergenerational, multicultural, and LGBTQI+ people from all over the world. We had skating parties and other fun activities.

My faith was built on love: serving a loving God, loving people, and living in God's transforming love. At church I developed life skills and honed my creativity as a singer, public speaker, teacher, and quilter with my Grandma Horton. I was a worship leader and sometimes opened the service with a prayer or a hymn. When I went to church as a child, I looked forward to the end of service when everyone would make a circle around the sanctuary and harmonize to the song, "Let There Be Peace on Earth." I would listen to the words of the song while looking around the room full of a diverse group of people and it really felt special. I loved going to First Church of Religious Science for that reason, God's love was all around me.

- How do you express your faith?
- Who helped you craft them?
- What is your first memory of experiencing God?
- How do you hold on to your faith?

Baptism

When I was twelve, I visited Mount Olive Baptist Church with my cousin Robin. At the end of the service, I felt the pull of God on my heart. I started to cry and when the pastor opened the doors of the church. I heard God say, "Get up."

I walked from the back of the church up front to the altar and shook the pastor's hand. Someone prayed with me, and I accepted salvation. When I opened my eyes I saw Robin, who was holding my hand. Someone I didn't know was holding my other hand. I was overwhelmed with emotion and through my tears saw a swarm of people standing around me. They pushed pamphlets into my chest inviting me to join their church clubs.

It was a lot to take in at that moment, but I was happy. I agreed to get baptized the next Sunday in the name of The Father, The Son, and the Holy Ghost. I gave my name and phone number to the church secretary, and she said, "I will call you on Saturday to tell you how to prepare for baptism."

That Saturday when I got the call from the church, my family was all together in the living room. When I hung up the phone, my daddy asked curiously, "What was that all about?"

"I'm getting baptized tomorrow, Daddy." I said excitedly.

My mom looked at me and smiled with pride. Daddy laughed and said, "I can baptize you upstairs in the tub." He and Uncle Marv laughed, but I didn't. "No, you can't, Daddy," I said confused. "The pastor has to do it."

My daddy wrinkled his face and asked, "Why do you want to get baptized?"

"So I can be a new creation." I was repeating what the pastor had said to me on Sunday.

"Oh?" he said. "And?"

"Well," I stumbled looking for words. "Then I can join the church." I didn't have the knowledge, or the understanding about baptism at the time. It was true that my father was qualified to baptize me. He told me he was "called to the ministry" when he was 21, but told God, "I ain't doing that sh-t!" As my father, he could have baptized me.

"You don't need to join that church to know God, girl. I am your daddy, Penn. I can baptize you. I am responsible to teach you how to live. I am to protect you and guide you." Daddy stood up and said, "Let's go upstairs." No, I didn't let my daddy baptize me in the bathtub. Now that he's gone, I wish I had.

I skipped baptism and never returned to Mount Olive Baptist Church. I did wonder if there was more to know about God. I wanted to know God on a deeper level, and I needed assurance of my faith. I started to search for Him.

Hell? Nah

A few weeks later, while hanging with my neighbors, my 12-year-old faith was called into question. "Do you believe in God?" my friend asked while her older sister braided my hair.

I looked down at the ground, up the street, then down the street and shook my head yes. "Yes, I believe in God. I go to church every Sunday with my whole family. I love church."

My friend asked, "Have you been baptized in the name of Jesus?" When my friend told me that I needed to be baptized in the name of Jesus, I was confused. The act of baptism was already new to me, but I had to choose which way was right.

"No. I was going to get baptized a couple weeks ago, but I changed my mind."

"Well," she said, emphatically, "If you haven't been baptized in Jesus' name, you're going to hell."

As the braiding sister pushed my head to the left to get a better grip, I felt air leave my lungs. "Go to hell?" I sighed, "What do you mean?"

"If you haven't accepted Jesus Christ as your personal Lord and Savior and been baptized in the name of Jesus, you are going to hell."

Up until that point, my faith was not restricted by fear, rules, or punishment. We didn't have strict, or rigorous religious standards at my church. Everywhere I looked, I saw God. I saw beauty and I felt butterflies on my shoulder.

I don't recall everything verbatim, but my friend said something like, "Sins are actions we do that don't please God. You know, when we break His rules, He's not happy with us."

I was perplexed. My God didn't have rules or inflict punishment on His children. "I really don't understand what ya'll are talking about," I squeaked.

I was fully convinced that I was God's child, but my neighbor stood up and said, "I'm going to get my mom so she can pray the prayer of salvation with you." I heard the screen door slam. A few seconds later it slammed again. My friend said, "Here's my mom."

The mother's slippers slid across the concrete porch. My head was bowed for the braid, but I saw her mother's slippers in front of me. "You don't have to go to hell, Penda," she said with compassion. "Do you want me to pray with you?"

I started to cry so hard that my body shaked. The idea of going to hell scared the hell out of me. Prior to that conversation, I was only aware of one side of God— His love. That girl introduced me to

His wrath. "It's okay, honey," she put her hand on my shoulder and said, "God loves you."

I repeated the words that she fed to me and invited God into my heart, again. The prayer felt different thank the first time. It replaced my former image of God for a God who needed me to please Him, which made me afraid of Him.

That night and for many nights after, I had nightmares about going to hell. When I think about it now, the part that hurts the most from that day is that I turned my face from God because I was terrified. I cared about my life and asked Him to save it, yet, for many years after that moment, I felt like I couldn't hit His mark of perfection. My perception of God was warped by my fear of displeasing Him.

My friends and their parents took me to their church. I didn't feel at home immediately. It was strict and I didn't recognize the spiritual languages, the dancing, or the reason I didn't get home until 11 p.m. that night. Truthfully, I was changed by that. I adopted the belief that God could only be found at a specific type of church which required me to act a certain way. What I didn't learn until I was an adult is that God was always with me. My friend Elyssa Schneider said confidently in an interview with me, "As Believers, we know that God is always going to be there. I do not walk alone."

This is when my quest to find God paralleled my father's search. We both wanted God. His understanding was "God Is All There Is "and mine was: "God is_____?" I came to an agreement with my father about God's love late into my forties. Shortly before he passed, I focused my faith on God's love for me, not his wrath. I regret that Daddy and I never got the chance to talk about what he taught me.

- What do you believe about God?
- What is your story of salvation?
- What is one situation that happened to confirm that God is real for you?

"When the winds and storms of life come with force, hold your position. You will be tossed and torn, but your feet are on a solid foundation— you will not break."

"Bend, Don't Break"
~Erica Laision, Interview

SEARCHING FOR GOD

By the time I was a junior in high school, our church had a new pastor. She was a Caucasian woman; that matters because it shifted the culture and changed how people related to each other. There weren't many people of color, and eventually, they moved to the suburbs, becoming a mostly White-cisgendered congregation. With that disruption to my church experience, I was left to find God on my own. Looking back, I can see the thread of God's faithfulness. He was there, even when I didn't recognize what He looked like.

I was looking for God, but my relationship with Him didn't feel the same as it had before my knowledge of hell. I could no longer see stars at night or feel God around me. I went to church, but didn't feel free, or safe. I fretted about my life before accepting salvation. I was worried about doing something wrong and going to hell. I became regimented, ritualistic, and could not see God outside of the tiny frame I constructed for Him.

I wanted to touch, feel, and see Him, but I was afraid. I wanted the butterfly back on my shoulder, the sweetness of peace and the unity of His people, but it was gone. I didn't couldn't retrieve it. I wrapped myself in procedures and policies trying to hold on to a façade of faith, but eventually I went flat, like a tire. I went from a young person with spiritual freedom, to a young adult bound by religion. I wish I had known what my friend Deidra taught me in an interview back then, "Faith is complete confidence and trust in God. I stand tall."

Mentored in Life and Faith

When I was 17, my mentor at the time, Lena, led me through the prayer of salvation for the third time. Lena had been talking to me about my walk with God for a while. She had been my mentor since I was 12 years old. We spent a lot of time together riding in the van going to different activities. I was open when I shared with her some of the life events that had shaped me. I talked to her about my family life, my aspirations, my disappointments, and my goals. I was carrying so much in my heart.

My soul was crying out for comfort in places that only God could touch. I had survived sexual abuse, lost friends to suicide, observed intimate partner violence, and been impacted by other people's alcoholism and drug abuse. I shared things in my life with her that I had not shared with my parents. I was conflicted by turning away from the family religion, and I misjudged them.

Lena introduced me to the God who had formed me in my mother's womb. The same God that knew my name and sent His son to die for me because He loved me so much. Those specific explanations of God made Him real to me again. When she asked if I was ready, I bowed my knees with tears in my eyes and surrendered. On December 17, 1991, in the basement of the West Dayton Boys and Girls Club—I felt completely changed in that moment.

I expected every mentor relationship to meet the standard that Lena and her husband, Horace set for me. They spent time with me which developed trust and made me an extended addition to their family. They invested their time, resources, and treasure into me from the time I was an adolescent until I became a young adult. I didn't know how to balance my love for them with my love for my parents. At times I chose one over the other, which created tension in those relationships. As a mom, I understand the importance of having a village. My child has relationships with people who love and support her; they would never betray her confidence or trust.

I do my best to "sow forward" what Lena and Horace poured into me. I will never be able to repay them for their contribution to my life. They taught me how to study my bible. They prayed with me, explained Biblical principles, and modeled for me how to live as a child of God. I love them deeply for what they gave me. Sadly, my newfound faith clashed with the theology that my daddy believed. I acted like I was a black sheep in my family, but I wasn't. I leaned on our family declaration that "God is All There Is," I just didn't know how to verbalize my faith effectively. If I had known what my friend Erica Lasion shared in an interview, "Hold on to God, no matter what," I would have been better at bending and not breaking much earlier in life.

A Lesson from my Daddy

When I was a junior in college, I went home for a hair appointment. When I got back, my father was watching a football game. He was having a bottle of beer. I must have rolled my eyes in disgust at the sight of him drinking, because my father, irritated with my reaction, said, "What's wrong with your face?"

"What do you mean?" I tossed my purse on the chair in front of me.

"I saw you turn your nose up. That's rude, Pen." Daddy flipped my purse on the floor, and pointed to the chair next to him, "Sit down." He snatched a beer from a box, twisted the cap off and handed it to me. He said, "Drink it."

I refused to take the bottle at first, "If you don't drink it," he held the bottle at the top of my freshly permed hair, "I'm going to pour it all over your head." I grabbed that bottle of beer before he could think twice and cradled it!

I caressed the sleek green bottle before taking a sip. The contents tasted like liquid dirt, and I whined at how much I didn't like it. I crossed my legs as if that would help me choke down the drink, but Daddy wasn't moved by my complaining, "Finish it."

It took me a couple of hours to consume the seven ounces of liquid in that bottle. It made me want to gag and I felt guilty for drinking it. When I was finished, my father held the bottle up to the light to check that I had consumed every drop, and then he tossed it into the trash can.

All I thought about was going upstairs to scrub my teeth and tongue with my toothbrush and some strong toothpaste. I had imagined feeling different from the alcohol, but I didn't feel anything.

I wasn't sick, my head didn't hurt, nor did I get sent to hell.

My father interrupted my thoughts when he said, "I don't want you to be the type of person who looks down on people, Penn. The greatest gift that God has given us is volition—the power to choose. Don't put yourself in God's place." I could see that he cared about what he was talking about. "Remember when you told me I was going to hell?"

Yes, I told my father that he was going to hell. After I got saved, I judged everything and everyone if they didn't look like what I thought a Christian should look like. One day I was doing my homework at the dining room table and my father came in from Happy Hour. He was so happy and full of joy, but I could smell alcohol on him.

I chuckled at the memory.

"It's not funny. I'll never forget that because it pissed me off so much." He sighed. "I want you to be able to talk to a janitor and a president of a company. I don't want you to offend people who are different from you or believe something different than you do. That's not who we are."

My personal convictions about drinking alcohol were shaped by the people I was around who were all "dry." I made a pledge not to consume alcohol as a teenager. I had seen some ill-effects of alcoholism such as when a classmate in middle school sprained his back at a party when he fell down the stairs drunk. I saw a woman try to stab herself in a drunken stupor.

I am not going to try to convince you to land on either side of the fence about alcohol, what I want you to think about is how I approached people and situations when alcohol was involved. I was unreasonable and unwavering in my stance about alcohol use around me. I was bold like I had been taught at church, and I said, "Daddy, if you don't stop drinking you are going to hell."

I was critical of anyone who drank alcohol because I went to a church that taught against consumption of it Immediately his demeanor changed, and he became livid. My daddy didn't talk to me for several days. I wasn't moved by his anger at the time because I believed that I was doing the right thing by calling out his "sin." It was wrong to say that to him. I was wrong for judging my daddy. I regret that moment.

Another moment that I regret is that I chose to have no alcohol at my wedding reception. I would not allow my parents to celebrate my nuptials with their friends in their way. If I could turn back time, I would have asked more questions, spoken more slowly and been more compassionate. I would have allowed daddy to party with his friends after I left. After that conversation with Daddy I went to bed, disgusted that alcohol had touched my lips. I probably prayed a long, heart filled and tear-laced prayer for God's forgiveness before falling asleep.

Bend, Don't Break

I heard what my father said about judgement, but I didn't digest it immediately. I remember having an internal battle about alcohol that day and that battle followed me into adulthood.

When I was in college at Wilberforce University, my friend Erica ("E") introduced me to GMWA Mass Choir's 1994 song, "Bend, Don't Break." Anytime she played it, she would act out the words by bending over and popping back up quickly. Our sister time has always spiritually and physically been rejuvenating in that way. I laughed at first, but she was saying something I would understand and apply in my life. I began to pantomime the words to that song whenever I needed a reminder that I am resilient.

I went to graduate school at Bowling Green State University which is only two hours from Elyria, Ohio. It was a country drive that relaxed and inspired me if I had a stressful week of studying, researching, and working three jobs.

When I arrived at E's house, I would climb the steps to her guest room and take a nap. Her guest room was my sanctuary because it was quiet, peaceful, and steeped in prayer. Sleeping at E's house always restored me in a way that I cannot explain. I would wake up and be charged up for sister time.

During one of my visits, I was so hungry, (maybe that was an indication that I was hungry for God). I made a turkey sandwich while E cooked. After she put the pan in the oven, she lit a cigarette and retrieved a bottle of red wine from the fridge. This was not unusual, but I must have been feeling extra self-righteous that day. I watched her choose a clear wine glass from the cabinet. She turned and asked, "Penn, you want a glass of wine?"

I think I wrinkled my nose and said, "You know I don't drink, Erica." I probably rolled my eyes too. E took a deep breath. She held her glass in one hand and cigarette in the other as she sashayed to the dining room table. I finished making my sandwich and sat opposite of her at the table. For a few seconds Erica looked around the room and the silence between us was cold. She took a drag of her cigarette and swirled the wine in her glass watching it spin. After taking a long drag, Erica said, "You didn't have to say it like that." My heart sank and I thought, "Oh no! That's what Daddy meant." I had done the exact same thing to E that I did to my daddy and I was ashamed.

What had happened with E was exactly what my father was trying to prevent me from doing. "That was rude," E sighed. "Once a week I smoke one cigarette and drink one glass of wine, Penn." I watched the smoke rise from her cigarette. "I'm sorry E, I don't like alcohol."

"That's fine, but don't look down on me because I do, Penn."

It took the weekend for me to process how much I had hurt Erica with my tone. I didn't mean to be judgmental; I was just trying to protect my own spirituality. I didn't know how to balance my beliefs at the time. I have ruminated on that experience for many years. Erica and I are still friends, she allowed me to grow into myself, but she kept me accountable about how I treated her. After that experience, I became more careful about how I reacted when people drank around me.

It's Not You, It's the Wine

I want to talk about my friend Jai Robin, she wrote a book, "Life Lessons, Journey to my Dopeness." In celebration of her divorce, Jai invited me to join her for a "Celebration of Life" dinner in 2016. She invited a group of her supporters, as she explained to "Celebrate my decision to live." I won't go into the details of Jai's personal story, if you want to know more about her, go read her book. What I do want to emphasize is that she went through hell. When she made it out of that fire, she chose her life. She moved from Pittsburgh back home to Philly in October of 2018.

When Jai called to invite me to dinner, I was excited. I had never been to a winery and that sounded like a great experience. I told her to reserve a spot for me, "No doubt," I told her, "I'll be there."

Sadly, when I mentioned the dinner invitation to my husband RJ, he told me I couldn't go. "You know you and Jai are going to take pictures."

"And?" I questioned.

"I'm trying to get a job. If the search committee sees you in a picture with a wine glass, I won't get this opportunity. Please, don't go."

"But you know I don't drink," I pouted.

One Christmas Eve my younger sister was driving my parent's van. She had gotten her license a few months before and when my friend, and her infant daughter needed to go home, she was excited to drive. We were stopped at a stop sign and had just inched into the intersection when a drunk driver ran the stop sign and t-boned us where I was sitting. My sister and my friend were crying hysterically, for obvious reasons.

I have seen how people become incapacitated from drinking too much alcohol and as a result, my choice was to refrain. The problem with that choice is that I did not have balance. I became self-righteous and judgmental about people who drink, lumping everyone into a category of abusers. I had not experienced enough life to understand that people can be responsible with alcohol, and that drinking was their choice.

"I know you don't drink," RJ sighed, "but they don't know that about you. Maybe you can celebrate with her another time. You know we are trying to get out of here, and I can't risk it right now. "I was crushed. I called my friend crying and told her I couldn't go. We made plans to have breakfast, but it was not the same as celebrating with a group.

That is one of the moments that I shrank into myself. I know it specifically because I remembered scrolling through social media and noticing an uptick of follow requests from people in a city I had never heard about. It dawned on me that I was already under a microscope because of RJ's job search. "They" were watching me. I froze in fear thinking about the strangers who were investigating me to determine my husband's next career move and the future of our family. I was concerned that they would find a reason not to choose him because of me. I had personal knowledge of a ministry couple who had experienced that situation.

As a result, I adopted the paradigm that I was not going to be accepted by them because I did not measure up to their standards. I went to the extreme of scrubbing all my photos. I silenced myself, turned my welcome light off and hung a sign on my heart: Sorry, I'm Closed. I had previously enjoyed the Periscope app and went live several times a day, but after RJ told me I couldn't go to the winery, I threw the invisible blanket of judgement over everything in my life. I interpreted his statement to say that people in the church would not want a first, lady with feelings or thoughts.

To no one, I made a sacred vow, "I won't be the reason my husband isn't able to walk into his destiny!" Even though I wanted to be there with my friend, I knew that it was futile to fight my husband's request, the cost was too high. If I chose to go to the dinner and got tagged in a photo and a wine glass was on a table, he might be disqualified for the jobs he applied for.

I felt like a helium balloon a few days after a birthday celebration. I was shrinking but it wasn't noticeable. I was worried that a group of people were going to determine my husband's destiny. I didn't want to mess up anything for him. If they saw a wine glass on a table in a picture, they weren't going to hire someone with a "drunkard, wayward, wife."

What they wouldn't have known, unless they asked me, is that a wine glass on a table wouldn't have been mine because I. Don't. Drink. If they had asked, I would have said, "I was celebrating my sister who chose not to take her life!" If they had asked, I would have told them how much it meant to be present for someone I loved when she wanted to celebrate life. I know the value of the ministry of presence. I often thought about that missed opportunity when I did not feel accepted or embraced by people at church.

I asked myself, "Penda, why are you exhibiting all of this emotion and confusion because of alcohol that you don't even consume?" My view of God changed again, this time because of someone else's point of view about me. That night, I took a deep breath, sucked in my optimism, and held it for six years.

I dared to share some of my own biases and judgements with you. Share some of your own biases, honestly, using the questions below.

- What are some of your deep convictions?
- If you had a disagreement with someone about something you believed, what happened?
- How did the disagreement impact your relationship?
- What are some biases you never speak out loud?

"No matter what, come what may, you have to get to the promise."

"I Press Through the Pain to Get to the Promise"
~Danada Beckwith, Interview

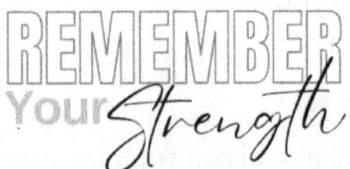

PRESS TOWARD THE MARK

2016.

This could be its own book; this heartbreaking year changed me. I limped through the year.

My mom and mother-in-law passed; my husband's paternal grandmother died unexpectedly. Our daughter spent almost two weeks in the ICU with an asthmatic episode. Two weeks later, a young child in my husband's family died from the same kind of asthma attack. The day after my husband interviewed at one of the churches he was applying to serve as pastor, his mother died.

Hit after hit. After hit.

On top of that, the violence in the neighborhood was heavy. There were several gruesome shootings in the Wilkinsburg, Pennsylvania neighborhood where we lived. I caught the bus to work so I walked a lot in the neighborhood. I was anxious because it was such an unpredictable time for the community. My husband resorted to dropping me off and picking me up from work which made me feel better.

During those daily drives, we had a lot of time to talk before we picked our daughter up from her after school program. We agreed that our time in Pittsburgh was ending. We were feeling the stretch of our roots growing, but we didn't have an open door to move anywhere else. We prayed and asked God to open a door for us to serve in ministry outside of Pennsylvania. Have you ever had to sacrifice something you wanted to do in the present for your future? That's why, when Jai Robin invited me to dinner at the winery, I understood why I couldn't go. During that time, I had several downloads for specific ministry ideas. I started carrying a notebook with me to record the cryptic notes:

- Ministry Fair and Directory of Ministries
- When moving to a new neighborhood do the police ride along, community leadership program, or find a priority board to get involved
- Create a women's summit. Brunch-style meeting. 23 sponsors who have applied to speak. Penda chooses the theme. Feature female Black entrepreneurs and have giveaways

- Senior Women's Ministry for those new to the faith or who have church hurt:
- groom their confidence and encourage them to let them teach and be taught.
- they can dance! (remember Ms. Cookie!)

A few weeks after Jai's dinner, which was also a few weeks after his mother's funeral, RJ got his dream job as a pastor. He breathed a sigh of relief and let his shoulders relax. As a wife, it was good to see my partner excited about something so precious to him.

I hoped and believed that life was going to change for us with this move. I didn't realize how my expectations for those changes were unrealistic and improbable. My unrealistic expectations became a problem for me.

I resigned from my job feeling mixed emotions. I had made great friends, and I loved many things about Pittsburgh. I was resigning from a job I had worked up the ranks to get hired for. I was interviewing for a position that was my dream job within the County, and I was four months away from getting vested in my pension, that was hard. I pushed down the emotions I was feeling because I knew this move was for the best. I loved my supervisor, Jean, because she was a great mentor and teacher. We shared a moment of reflection and a few tears. I was part of a team that reviewed child fatalities and I loved that job, but I was sad, yet I was happy to have been part of such a powerful team. "We've been praying for this change," I told my supervisor.

My last day of work with the county was December 9, 2016. My team sent me off with a bang by giving me a departmental going away party. I made it through that day, but it was emotional. I started packing up my life in Pittsburgh the next day. I purged everything because I was eager to start over in every way. A few weeks later I took what I could carry, for me and my daughter, in two suitcases and boarded a plane.

I didn't have the awareness of how to turn the part of my personality off that was trained to be critical. I moved from reviewing cases looking at risk factors to critiquing my family, friends, and any place I visited. I was always mentally creating safety plans and looking for risk factors.

Welcome Home!

Walking through the airport I felt the apprehension of the unknown. I gripped my then nine-year-old daughter's hand and dragged our carry-on. We greeted my husband at the arrival gate and went to baggage claim. When we saw RJ, my daughter let my hand go and ran to her father. Watching them hug, I felt relieved. "We are home," I thought. That moment played over and over in my mind for weeks. A daughter, running into the arms of her father and him swooping her up in a tight embrace. I needed the visual reminder on days when I felt a chasm of distance between me and God. I needed God because my shell was cracked.

I looked forward to working in ministry.

*"I am set on purpose.
I have a resolution to live
my life according to
God's values."*

"I am Resolute."
~Charice Manor, Interview

BE RESOLUTE

I was optimistic. I had high expectations about my new life in ministry leadership. I had my little notebook full of ideas and years of experience serving people. I was ready to get my hands dirty with work. Everybody knows that a new person can't just go in and make changes. So, for a year, I sat still, taking notes and trying to get the lay of the land in our new environment.

Those first few months in our new state we had to cover household expenses and needs with our personal credit cards. I hated having to do that because I had saved money, and my credit card had a zero balance before we moved. To fit the standard, I had to buy all new clothes and keep my appearance pristine, for the different level.

Making the Adjustment

I spent the first few months building the foundation of my business as a writing coach. I was engaged in my full-time entrepreneurship and being a stay-at-home mom and wife. Someone recommended a non-profit that was looking for volunteers and I got involved quickly. For three years I volunteered a couple times a week.

I took a personality assessment to identify my gifts and how I could serve at the church. Part of the process included taking the DISC personality assessment. My results of the DISC assessment were that I am high "COMPLIANT" or a high "C." The description confirmed that I am introverted, cautious, careful, and picky. Before hearing my DISC results, I was thinking that my attention to detail, and criticism of systems was a character flaw instead of a gift.

Although I wanted to open up to everyone, I couldn't trust a lot of people with my thoughts, feelings, or experiences. My introverted nature didn't help people get to know me, either. I was stuck between a rock and a hard place trying to stretch my roots while grieving. Most times, my grief kept me distant. I trusted God, but I wondered if I was shut in the lion's den.

Before my husband became a pastor, I had been a member of four churches total in my life. From the time I was seventeen I was active in congregations: serving as a greeter, singing in the choir, volunteering with the youth, or writing for the magazine.

I was taught that I needed to serve in my local congregation which helps it to fulfill its mission. During those days, I went to church several times a week for meetings, services, activities, and prayer. My contacts, connections, and resources were mostly church-related, and I expected that to be what our new church would offer my family.

I expected to be around people who would help me heal from the pain I carried from losing my mother. Honestly, no one but God could have supplied what I wanted and needed, them for me.

The misunderstanding festered and hardened until it created a wedge that separated me from other people. I wanted so badly to be an example and to give my all to the new environment, but I was misunderstood on so many levels. The misunderstanding and cultural differences were a factor, but I was the one who was acting entitled.

According to the American Heritage Dictionary, the definition of entitlement is to furnish with a right or claim to something. In a sermon entitled "Triggers: Entitlement" by John Hannah, I learned another definition. He explained, "Entitlement comes from jealous behaviors. Expectation means that you are owed something. Emptiness means that you are missing something, and Entitlement means that you have the right to something." Essentially, I falsely believed that I had to have privileges or special treatment because I was the pastor's wife.

I wanted special treatment, but it wasn't about people throwing flowers at my feet or parting the red sea when I entered the room. I wanted to be protected when I felt unsafe, because I often was confronted by members who didn't like my husband or community members who missed the former pastor. I wanted to be listened to when I spoke up, I had a lot of ideas and at times, as soon as I opened my mouth, I was shut down by someone saying, "we don't do it that way."

My misunderstanding of how other pastor's wives were treated created a false reality. I didn't want my husband to worry about money, or never be able to get the rest he needs because he worked so hard. For my young daughter to never walk the halls of the church unescorted and to be allowed to share and implement the vision that God had given me to help broken, rejected, and neglected church members. I was impatient with God and tried to get Him to move how, when, and in the way I wanted Him to. I thought my mustard seed faith was enough to manipulate God. I thought that it would be natural for me to mesh with the congregation, but I didn't learn the culture quickly enough and my entitlement, or false expectations created barriers between me and people who wanted to get to know me.

What I experienced at my prior churches isn't normal in most churches. The pastors' wives around me did not understand my experience. They were all either working in tandem with their husbands as copastors of their churches, or maintained full-time employment, participating in ministry on the weekends. My life was different, I had given up so much and their lack of understanding caused me to feel isolated.

There were so many things I wanted to process, but I couldn't talk about it to anyone. If I shared my feelings with RJ, he felt that he couldn't talk to me if I expressed emotion. I needed to remain a safe place for my husband. My reaction was to absorb my emotions and his. I couldn't have close relationships with anyone. I really didn't know all of the people who were truly for me, so I kept my circle small. I created a shell to protect myself, but what I thought about how people felt about me wasn't completely true.

I was open and authentic when I showed up, but I was judged for how I walked, what I wore, how my hair was styled, what I said, and who I said it to. People accused me of being distant and unfriendly.

Someone even said about me, "She is not a good representative for him" meaning my husband, their pastor. I couldn't please them, and I expended a lot of time, energy and tears trying.

My cryptic journal notes continued:

- Form a women's ministry from Strengths Based Family Worker (SFW Class) – How would things be? What are we working toward? This is an example of a Miracle Question
- Small businesses to rent space
- Explain how communion works to visitors
- Survey members
- Welcome Ministry – Be welcoming to visitors from every entry point; that is important
- For New Year's Eve Service – give a new year charge. A theme or instructions for the house
- Create a packet for new residents
- Mommy and Me Outing
- Baking
- Paint and Sip

I knew that I was being watched. Not like someone watching me walk past them at the mall. More like I was sitting in a glass bowl, and someone was binge-watching every episode to find out what happens next. Although I tried to maintain some level of privacy, I was constantly questioned about e-ve-r-y-thing. It felt like I was under a microscope.

From December 2016 until April 2017, when my husband's official installation service was scheduled, life moved quickly for us. Everything I did to prepare for my husband's installation celebration was about other people, and not me.

Not God.

Our family and friends came from all over the country in April of 2017 to celebrate my husband's installation as a pastor. I was so happy to have all of our loved ones near us, but when the celebration was over, I wasn't feeling like myself anymore. Slowly, I stopped recognizing myself. In pictures from that time, I am hidden behind a hat that belonged to my mother-in-law. I didn't know how to wear the hat correctly and it is evident in the photos.

My sister-in-law and I both wore one of her hats to the funeral. The family decided that I needed to wear one of her favorite blue hats. That hat represented her love for style and, because it is large, was a symbol of the role I would soon have as a Pastor's wife. It wasn't representative of me, but I loved her, so I wore it for her. For his installation, I wore her hat to have a piece of her with me. (If you want to know more, I shared in detail about the Installation Service in a previous book, *First, Lady: Called, Confident, and Committed Woman in Leadership*.)

By July I knew I needed to work harder to fit in. Something was wrong, but I didn't know how to communicate what I needed. As a pastor's wife, I couldn't be open with everyone who wanted to be close to me; it was hard to explain why. I constantly questioned other people's intentions and motives and they were questioning me. It was a constant tug of war. No one that I talked to understood what I was going through, even other pastor's wives. I made a list of questions to ask other pastor's wives and started trying to build a village:

- How do you deal with rejection?
- How do you practice your self-care?
- How do you create the atmosphere?
- Are you involved in any ministries?
- How do you define leadership?
- Who are your mentors?
- How did you know you could trust them?
- What are your expectations of people?
- How do you get ministered to?
- Do you visit or stay at one church?
- Define confidence versus arrogance?

I tried several times to open myself up and I did with a small group of people. I needed support but I wasn't finding it in the places I was looking. There were people who rose up to support my family. They know who they are, and I love them deeply for how they stood with me. This gratitude runs deep.

Without their support, I might have folded under the constant attacks on my character, integrity, and intentions. The attacks on my husband made me weary. I was always ready to go to battle because I had to defend myself. It wasn't about having thick skin to let things roll off my back, it was about preserving the integrity of my name—my daddy named me, and I wanted to keep its reputation intact.

Boxes

I've always been beautiful, my daddy told me so
But some days
I forgot to remember
and acted like I didn't know.

Come Back, Daughter

God was calling me back to where I first loved Him. I didn't see it at the beginning, and I had to circle around the mountain several times before I understood that God wanted to humble me. I have been involved in ministry with my husband for over 20 years. Like my friend Tiffany Countryman says, "Ministry is me and my life is ministry." In every season, He has pruned me and shaped me. When I surrendered to the call my heartache subsided. But I didn't fully surrender my will until four years later.

Everything that I knew about myself was becoming unrecognizable and I didn't like it. At every turn I was constantly fighting to demonstrate my significance, but I was isolated and rejected because their standard for me was higher than I could reach. I found in a journal a statement I had written years earlier, "Be a dandelion, resilient and fulfilling purpose even when people only see you as a weed."

Not one time did I ask God to confirm His standard so I could reach it. I took my eyes off of Him and turned toward the approval of His people. I was striving to serve people, lead them with love, and be a source of inspiration, but I was bumping my head against a church tradition and culture that was new to me.

In the church I felt like an exchange student who was visiting a foreign country. I didn't speak the language of the majority. I didn't understand some of the beliefs or the historical implications of some of the traditions. In any environment it takes time to learn new things, and, in some situations, there is a teacher to help facilitate the student's learning.

I was on my own.

Breaking My Fast

When my husband and I were dating, I chose Sunday as a day to abstain from food and drink whenever he had a ministry assignment. At the time we attended and served in different churches. If he had to preach and I couldn't be physically present, fasting was a way for me to unite with him in prayer. By the time he became a shepherd, I had been fasting on Sundays for 16 years. My daddy taught me that dressing well translates to how I act, respond, and interact with the people around me. When I would get dressed for church, I made sure I put on an outfit that made me feel good and look good. I was doing fine until people started complaining about my clothes.

That is why it was hard for me to be surrounded by people with loving intentions who wanted to meet me and talk to me immediately after service. I know my husband's habits, mannerisms, and when a word was heavy for him. If I knew he was wrestling to deliver a particular theme or message, my senses were heightened. People didn't understand my silence in those moments.

I could not realistically ever give 100% of my attention to meeting people, kneeling to gatekeepers of the church, or answering a lot of questions on a Sunday after church. People would be so agitated with me if I didn't remember their name. Someone said to me, "I've told you my name several times. Our former leader and his wife knew everyone by name," and then she stormed away in a huff.

One Sunday I was wearing a wrap skirt, and my knot was loose. I sat down in a pew to fix it and people stood around waiting to talk to me. I asked someone to stand in front of me because if I got up my skirt would have unraveled and that would have been a terrible wardrobe malfunction. A woman who was waiting to talk to me said, "I like your outfit, today." From that moment, I made sure to never be by myself. But there was always a complaint about the person or persons who were with me.

When invited to lunch or breakfast meetings, I would ask people to meet me at the park instead. I would invite them to volunteer with me. It was not ideal for people to get to know more about me in an environment that was not native to me.

After service, people would take their anger and frustration out on me if my husband said or did something that upset them. All I could do was stand there and take it on the chin. Standing stoically, I would chew and swallow the insults, judgement, anger, and frustration that was tossed at me. It was better to eat the words than speak out of line and risk offending someone and making matters worse. Proverbs 18:21 says, "Death and life are in the power of the tongue: and they that love it shall eat the fruit thereof" (KJV).

I could relate to the Biblical illustration of Daniel in the lion's den. I was sitting in the face of lions but trusting God to keep His promises. I knew that I belonged there. My friend Beth Ruffin taught me that when she said in an interview, "Stop waiting around for people to see your value. Recognize your value for yourself and step up."

It takes trust in God to be in the presence of lions, especially when you know what they are capable of. Faith kicks in when you know that because you are God's child, the lions won't attack you. They may not attack, but the cave will be dark. It will be cold, and you'll hear the lions breathing. I couldn't fight the lions. Neither can you.

If it wasn't one thing it was another; I was always perceived as being in the wrong. I was in a place that did not allow me to be fully me.

After one incident when someone walked up to my daughter (who was nine at the time) and demanded that she greet her by name, I was livid. The woman did not greet my daughter by her name yet demanded that she greet her with a title. My child had never met this person before. When I saw how this action had hurt my child, my bear claws came out whenever this elder was around. There were actions that reminded me of her: a person touching my daughter's hair without her permission, another person demanding that she speak to them, a group of women rolling their eyes at her when she walked past them. Every Sunday my head was on a swivel, watching, praying, guarding my heart.

I wrote in my journal:

Lady Penda.

There is a separation and I need to walk in it. God has a standard He wants us to reach here. He is using me. Someone said, "The whole church is looking at you what are you going to do?"

I knew that in order to protect my child, I needed to raise my standard of discernment and at the same time try to assimilate in the culture, or I was going to get devoured.

I became frustrated and my disappointment led me to treat people differently. The self-absorbed mentality I had was based in the same judgement I once felt about people drinking alcohol. I knew it meant that I was out of alignment with God, but I didn't identify it instantly.

Instead, I started to feel dismissed and minimized. But Deuteronomy 31:5 reminded me otherwise:

Be strong and of good courage, do not fear nor be afraid of them; for the LORD your God,
He is the One who goes with you.
He will not leave you nor forsake you."
(NKJV)

Pushing Myself Aside

The process of losing helium, like a balloon, was long and slow. By the third year, being married to Pastor in a place that did not embrace me, I had shut down every part of myself that brought me joy. I was like the birthday balloon tied to a chair that everyone had forgotten about. It was pretty, but under the table, scratching the floor. I was quitting on myself, and RJ would say, "Come on, my wife, keep fighting. Forget the environment that you may be operating in right now. Be yourself. I'm here, I will protect you."

I would shake my head and say, "I don't want to. I don't want to operate in the excellence that I know I'm supposed to be operating in." I wanted to get my air back, but I felt that in that environment, it was safer for me to hang low.

RJ planted seeds of encouragement in me by saying, "Get back up, pick up your mantle and keep running without stopping until you get to the end." His words stayed with me even though I acted like I didn't hear him.

He would say, "Now is not the season for you or our family to quit on the things that God has called us to do. There are people who need to hear from you that only you can reach. Especially during this season. Opposition comes when your breakthrough is right around the corner." I was inspired when RJ said, "We have been broken a lot.

In ministry we go through things to better prepare us for service to others."

On the other side of the brokenness I felt, I now realize how people can be broken in many ways. For me, resilience was tied to my faith and that kept me going. When I didn't recognize it, there was something in me that stirred me to thrive. Sometimes the warrior in me didn't know what she was fighting for, all she knew was that she did not want to die in that place.

I wanted to leave everything I had on the floor like a dancer, and when I could, I did.

When Reality Sets In

I am the effect of my choices, the patterns I rejected or accepted
The woman on my vision board is slowly manifesting
Does she still have time to flow through the birthing canal of fantasy into my reality?
Reality reminds me, time is not waiting for me to decide.

- What do you believe is true about you? (This is your strength).
- What actions have you taken to further validate/affirm these truths?
- On a scale of 1-10, where is your strength right now? Are you weak right now?
- What are you doing either way to remember your strength?
- How can you start building your strength?

"I did not understand that my strength did not exist in the same way it had before."

"The world came crashing in on me . . . either get living, or you get dying. Living after the snap was my bread crumbs to living higher."

"I Live After the Snap"
~Kian Furnace, Interview

STAY IN THE BUBBLE

On March 11, 2020, the World Health Organization declared the COVID-19 virus a global pandemic. The existence of this disease, prevalent across the globe, forced life as "normal" to change. Rituals were upended, routines suspended, and expectations were twisted as stay-at-home mandates, quarantines, and mask-wearing were regulated. Social distancing – the necessity of remaining six feet apart, became a new normal and the current mode for interacting with others. Individuals who were in quarantine together did not intermingle with people outside of their safety zones, or "bubble."

Mental health awareness and plans to support people living alone were given widespread attention. For some families, being together in quarantine opened up a new world of commitments, home school responsibilities, and learning how to balance work-life while being at home. No one expected or could have predicted how the COVID-19 pandemic would change the economy, the job market, family structures, or the entertainment industry.

Most people remember March 13, 2020, as the day that everyone was sent into quarantine, but it was the day after my 46th birthday. My family was out having pizza to celebrate. As soon as we finished eating, my daughter's school called to inform us that school was canceled the next day. Going into the bubble for COVID-19 is a metaphor for the healing season that was next to come in my life.

The COVID-19 virus came out of nowhere and ripped through the world furiously. A lot of people were knocked off their feet. We reevaluated our lives, our habits, our careers, our purpose. What we thought was going to be a short-term inconvenience turned out to be a worldwide pandemic. One day at home turned into two years of systematic and societal change.

With multiple variants, it has caused millions of civilian deaths worldwide, caused a mass exodus of employees from service-based jobs, and knocked the Black and Brown communities to their knees.

Several writers deemed the year 2020 as the year from hell. (Adam Gopnik, 2020; Jackie Salo 2020; Dr. Karsonya Wise Whitehead, 2020) In his New Yorker article entitled, "Our Year In Hell," Adam Gopnik wrote, "Throughout the year, nothing was normal, and everything seemed normalized."

Not only was there a pandemic, but major cultural events took place as well. In 2020 Kobe Bryant, his daughter, and several other precious souls were killed in a helicopter crash on their way to basketball practice. The president was impeached, Prince Harry and Meghan Markle left the royal family, and there was a stock market crash. On top of that, several major social justice events occurred in 2020 including nationwide Black Lives Matter Protests after the deaths of George Floyd, Ahmaud Arbery, and Breonna Taylor.

In August of 2020, Chadwick Boseman, best known for his work in Black Panther, 42 and Get on Up, died of cancer; the public/his fans did not know about his diagnosis. He was living and giving us his best work and I was keeping myself in a cave, peering out to give people what I thought they wanted because I was concerned about their opinions about me.

The year 2020 was difficult on many levels for all of these reasons. Dr. Karsonya Wise Whitehead mused: in her article, "2020: The Year from Hell":

> "Every country seems to be leaning in to help their citizens except us. We have received one stimulus check as an eviction crisis is

happening, as small businesses are closing, as our children are being educated from our kitchen tables, as our positive case numbers are rising, and as incomes are falling. Our politicians are playing politics as millions of us struggle to pay our bills. I have never been so disgusted and frankly embarrassed to be an American." (December 31, 2020)

The impact of social uprisings was reflected in entertainment as people used their phones to record and share injustices in real-time. With so many clashes of morals, values, ideals, and motivations, where was culture supposed to go and how was it supposed to respond to the shift in the standard? It had to find a way to make its imprint and it showed up in films. In an article listing the top 15 social impact films of 2020, the writers penned this statement:

> "The year 2020 was one of the loud and urgent calls for societal change, as the country's racial and economic divides were starkly exposed by both the COVID-19 pandemic and the most unconventional presidential campaign of our lives. The best social impact films and television shows of

2020 put the issues that traumatize, divide, unite and inspire us squarely at the heart of their narratives" (USC School of Cinematic Arts Staff, 2020).

Some of the films listed in the USC School of Cinematic Arts Staff article that highlighted social justice issues included a documentary about John Lewis "Good Trouble," a documentary about transgender representation "Disclosure," and Chadwick Boseman's last film, "Ma Rainey's Black Bottom." The latter was written and published by August Wilson, a Pittsburgh born and bred writer.

Song writers AKLESSO and Gawvi wrote a song called "Worst Year" and to me, these three lines summed up my feelings about 2020:

> *"Ya I know it felt like everybody worst year ya . . .*
> *Wanted all the things that I prayed for*
> *But then knew God*
> *I wanted way more . . ."*

Major Surgery

For years I had experienced severe pain during my menstrual cycles. There were so many symptoms of fibroid tumors such as facial hair and a protruding stomach, but medical doctors did not test me for the issue until I moved down south. By that time, I was numb with pain for several days during the month. My tumors were so large that I had to have a bilateral bikini line incision to remove them and my uterus.

Starting in January 2020 I embarked on a personal healing journey to prepare for my surgery. I allowed myself to grieve because I had hoped to have more children. I wondered if having my uterus removed would mean that I could no longer dream. It may sound silly; I related nurturing my dreams to carrying a baby in my womb.

Then my father called and gave me an assignment to go the hospital to see about his first cousin . . .

A Moment of Reflection

In January of 2020, my father called me and told me that his first cousin, Luvenia was in the hospital. Their generation of cousins was close like blood siblings, so Daddy instructed me, "Go see Vennie. You gotta represent me."

I was scheduled that morning to support a church member whose father was being taken off of life support. I wanted to be in both places, but I chose to fulfill my father's request. I knew Vennie and loved her deeply because she was family, but we weren't close. I didn't get to spend a lot of time with her growing up.

When I got to the hospital I ran into our cousin, George, and his wife Sharon C on the elevator. Daddy and Vennie's first cousin Sharon A was there from Ohio. We all walked to Vennie's room, and I prayed for her. Touching Vennie to pray, I noticed that her body was cold. I didn't know her cold temperature meant that she was in a medically induced coma.

George's sister, Gwen came to the hospital a little later. I sat in a corner and listened to the ladies talk. It disappointed me that I had been so wrapped up in my own hurts, mostly self-created, about church, while I was missing out on so much life happening around me. Vennie lived 25 miles away from me and I hadn't tried to spend time with her.

Cousin Sharon A sniffed as she talked, "Vennie called to tell me she was dying." She paused, held back tears, and said, "She asked me to get here, but I couldn't fly out immediately." We talked about life and Sharon told me to get my painful cycles checked. I told them I was going to have a hysterectomy. In that moment I was sitting at the feet of my elders, gathering wisdom.

I noticed that from the moment Sharon arrived at the hospital, she did not leave Vennie's side. I watched her pace the room, pray, cry, strategize, think. She was focused and using her grief to fuel her actions. When I got home, I cried as I wrote this poem about their sisterhood, an experience I didn't have as the oldest grandchild on both sides of the family:

Don't Leave Me (2020)

She said, "Don't leave me."

Black women huddled in her hospital room, sobbing in disbelief that she was leaving them.
Reminiscing about her love.
I stared at the pink polish on her feet

Beautiful are the feet of those who bring good news.
This is the magnet who drew our family together.
Dying.
From cancer three weeks after learning of her diagnosis.
She knew it was happening, "Don't leave me."

They didn't.

As I tried to contain my grief of losing Vennie, I listened to my cousins, her sisters speak candidly about their connection. We talked about how Black women don't take care of ourselves when we experience pain. We talked about sisterhood, responsibilities, and staying connected to family.

I saw my cousins hold Vennie's hand. We cried and prayed together. I wasn't there when they called the time, but I left the hospital with conviction. I said to myself, "I haven't been to a family reunion since I was in middle school. I don't even have anyone I can call a sister-cousin." I recognized the power in their bond, and it reminded me that I need to reach out to my extended family much more.

Thinking about Vennie led me down a rabbit hole of emotions. Then, I found an email from my father dated February 15, 2015, after my mother's mastectomy. I had asked him, "What can I do to support you now? How is this impacting you? Do you feel that she is not the same woman?"

My dad responded in his message:

> *"She sees herself as a survivor and not a role model. She has gone through a lot, and she thinks she is alone in her suffering. She doesn't understand that WE ALL are going thru [sp] this with her. I see*

the pain and I try my best to make her feel comfortable. I do not bother her and yes, she does feel less than a complete woman, I can tell but she will not say that it affects her psyche-but it does."

I agreed with him, and I thought about my femininity. I began to develop rituals for my daily selfcare which included drinking a cup of hot tea every morning in my special mug. I bought new pajamas, took a walk for at least 30 minutes three times a week, and started making sure I was in bed by 10:00 p.m. I made soothing pedicures with peppermint oil and hot stones part of my ritual and most importantly, spent quiet time with God.

Every Monday morning at 6:00 a.m. I would pray with a prayer group or with friends. I read the book The Courage To Heal by Laura Davis and completed the accompanying The Courage to Heal Workbook. I was watering my roots so I could stand in my strength. Confronting my history of trauma was the first step of that process.

My procedure was supposed to be in April 2020, but I pushed it back to June 16, 2020, because of the pandemic. My husband drove me to the hospital at 5:00 a.m. He had to drop me off curbside because visitors were not allowed. I walked to the registration desk, feeling alone.

Time to Recover

For recovery I was confined to the couch for two months. I couldn't get into my bed because it was too high. Many church members were gracious and kind with their well wishes. When I was in the healing process, I had to be still. One of my favorite scriptures is Psalm 46:10, "Be still and know that I am God," I could not have any sudden movements with that abdominal incision. My physical healing process led to healing emotionally and spiritually.

The surgery was a literal example of what happened to help me heal. Up to two years after my hysterectomy, my core was healing. How I walked, slept, ate, and moved for eight weeks was limited. Eighteen months after my surgery I tried to pick up a heavy weight when exercising and pulled a muscle in my abdomen. That had me flat on my back for a week. It was a hard lesson that major surgery changes your body. I did not understand that my strength did not exist in the same way it had before. My muscles needed to be retrained so my strength could be resuscitated.

As it was with me after surgery, so it was when I began the process of remembering my strength. Then, I studied resilience. My friend Dr. Monique Robinson said something in an interview that resonated with me, "I Will Not Quit On Myself, Again. To quit is to constantly make excuses not to seal the deal."

- How do you define strength?
- When you are not okay, how easy is it for you to admit that you need to take a beat to regroup?
- How would you describe your experience living through the pandemic?
- Have you ever had surgery? What was your recovery process like?

Then Samson prayed to the Lord, "Sovereign Lord, remember me.

Please, God, strengthen me just once more . . ."

Judges 16:28 (NIV)

"Surrender is not this place that God is trying to get you to arrive at. Surrender is a journey that God is trying to get you to commit to walking out with Him."

"I am In Pursuit of Surrender."
~Angelique Strothers, Interview

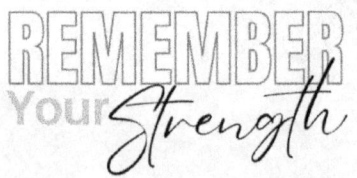

STRETCH OUT AND LET GO

In February of 2021, my family moved from one side of our city to another. I was causally talking to my friends Diana and Angelique about the move, and they agreed that I needed to spend time with God. "Allow Him to heal you before you leave the old house," Diana said. "You can't take all of that hurt with you. You need to admit that you are mad at God."

Resilience was calling my name and using my friends as vessels. Even though I refused to admit that I was anxious and having panic attacks at church, I had no choice but to answer its call. The heaviness of everything was crushing my resolve. After months and months of the "normal" way to pray, my prayers changed to one word. "Peace." "Rest." "Hope." "Love."

I was yearning for something more from God, and my decision to make life perfect made me obsess about things I could not control. I was walking with Him, and I felt my strength leaking out of me, again. Deep down inside, I clung to a hope that God loves me, but I didn't have the energy to walk in faith toward Him. If I, or someone did something unusual, or was opposite of what I would have done, I would ask myself, "Am I really a Christian?" It made me think of a statement my sister, Joi said during an interview, "Don't let anyone blow out your candle flame. Protect your heart and you'll be strong all the way through. Turn your glow up." The truth is, I needed God, but I was mad at Him. Instead of running toward God, I cowered in fear of Him. I didn't know how to ask for help. I was a First Lady sitting in a seat of leadership feeling isolated and rejected. My soul was wounded.

"The Bible says be anxious about nothing," I told my friends, trying to convince them that I was okay. They saw right through my façade. With their support I admitted my truth, "When we pull into the parking lot my heart races, my mouth gets dry, and I can't catch my breath."

"He can take it," Angelique reassured me. "Let God know how you feel."

Diana said, "If you need to cry, scream, cuss, kick, or punch. God can take it, but this new house is a fresh start for all of you."

"Yeah, Lady P," Angelique said. "Surrender this to God." When my expectations for how people were to treat my husband were not met, I rebelled against them and God. I started dreading Sundays.

Diana said. "Empty out, Penda."

I promised them, "I will make time to pray before we move. I already have a worship playlist. I will "Empty Out" because I have to learn how to hide myself in God and not hide from Him." Well, I sat down on my bed and thought I was emptying out, but my true release occurred a few months later, in our new home.

Empty Out

The empty out moment happened a few days after Jai's book signing. I truly saw myself in the mirror. I had just gotten out of the shower and put on my robe. I looked in the mirror to pluck at chin hairs. What I saw surprised me.

I shook my head in disbelief. "Ugh!" I thought. "You look awful."

The woman in the mirror had blazing red eyes with black tire marks around them that made me dizzy. Her head rested on her chest, its gravitational pull dragging her spine and shoulders in an unnatural curve. Her hair, although freshly washed, looked like dry pine needles.

"Hey." I waved in the mirror. "You alright?" I asked in confusion by the heaviness of the image I saw looking back at me.

I shrugged, looked at myself, and back down at my chest. "I don't know."

"What do you mean, you don't know?"

I looked down at the floor and nibbled on my fingernail, "I don't know." I paced the room searching for answers. Finding none in the circles I walked, I turned back to the mirror and said, "What happened to you? I me . . I mean…" I stammered, at a loss for words.

I glared at myself. "What?"

"What do you mean what?" That pissed me off. "Lady. . ."

I stopped myself and rolled my eyes, "Just leave it alone." Having a conversation with myself, I started to encourage myself. "I can't leave this alone. That's literally impossible."

I crossed my arms, let out a hard sigh and spoke, "You know what made me this way." I squinted my eyes to spray imaginary fire and said, "What you see is what you get."

"I don't recognize you anymore." I shrugged my shoulders and said nothing for a minute or two. I looked at myself and said aloud, "I've changed. But I'm still . . ."

I put my hand on my hip and tapped my foot. The healing me and the wounded me were facing off in the mirror. I kept my eyes on the mirror as I said,

"It is crucial to learn from your mistakes so you can heal."

"I haven't had time to heal," I thought. "But I can't make excuses for letting myself get this bad." I swallowed tears. "I'm sorry."

I remembered that in college someone made me look up the definition of the word 'Sorry' in the dictionary. Sorry means "worthless," and I try to never use that word.

"I ain't worthless," I said with authority. I still believe that is one truth about myself." "Good," the woman in the mirror said. "Penda, get your voice back, girl."

I pulled the belt of my plush white robe tightly around my waist and tied it into a sloppy bow. I said while looking in the mirror, "I'm so exhausted from all of this fighting." I wiped tears from my wet cheeks and said, "I feel so alone."

My heart said, "You're not alone."
I put some Vaseline on my cracked lips and rubbed them together. "Ah, that feels good," they said. "You've been neglecting us."

My shoulders said, "You can lean on other people sometimes. Why do you always have to be the strong one?" Every part of my body joined the conversation. I thought about when my friend Soleil said, "Every part of me that is hurting deserves to be healed." My eyes took in the sight of myself, and I knew I needed a makeover.

I inhaled, let my breath out slowly, and said out loud, "Your strength is the result of what you believe. What you believe determines your actions. Do you believe that you are strong right now?"

My whole self said, "Not yet, but I am ready to heal the pieces of me that have splintered."

I began to speak my truth out loud in the mirror. I thought about my mother, my grandmothers, and every story of resilience I could recall. With every recollection of a name or a victory from someone I loved, I gathered my strength. The experience of facing myself in the mirror brought four realities to my mind:

1. A confession that I was out of alignment
2. A series of conversations loved ones that required me to listen to them and record their bounce back stories for them and for myself
3. A personal rebranding process
4. The restoration of my faith

"Lord," I cried, "I put myself into a coffin and hid there. I repent for allowing my fear to be greater than my faith." I left the bathroom and laid down on my bed. It was time to do what Diana and Angelique had instructed, I had to empty out.

I turned on my Empty Out playlist and the first song was: "I Am Your Song" by Jonathan Nelson. God carefully put me into the pot of cold water. "The One" by Anthony Evans played next. "For Your Glory" by Tasha Cobbs started to turn the heat up. "Worship Medley" by Tye Tribbett came on, then the recording of my friend LaToya singing a medley at my mom's funeral took me deeper.

My worship was wet, sloppy, and beautiful at the same time. I didn't care what I looked like, I was being made whole, strengthening my shell as I let go of everything that was keeping me bound.

I don't know how long I was in that posture, but I remember hearing my Grandma Horton's voice, "Remember Your Strength." I chanted that phrase until I could no longer hear music. I got up from my bed leaving an imprint of my face in the soaking wet sheets. My tears had baptized me into a new beginning. "Remember your strength…"

I repeated. "Remember your strength. . ." Those words pulsated through my body like an electrical charge. That was a rite of passage— a moment that solidified a change in me. I got up from my bed, washed my face, fixed my hair, and went outside for a walk. As soon as I opened the door, I was greeted by a blue butterfly on a bush. I felt God all around me. It all boils down to love. Leading with love, honoring love, trusting love – this is my portion and my goal.

And the Lord answered me, and said, Write the vision, and make it plain upon tables, that he may run that readeth it.

For the vision is yet for an appointed time, but at the end it shall speak, and not lie: though it tarry, wait for it; because it will surely come, it will not tarry.

Habakkuk 2:2-3 (KJV)

The Result (2018)

I am the effect of my choices,
the patterns I rejected or accepted
The woman on my vision board is manifesting slowly

Does she still have time to
flow through the birthing canal of fantasy into my reality?
Reality reminds me, time is not waiting for me to decide.

> *"If I am in alignment with where I am supposed to be, everything I need is there."*

"I Will Finish It"
~Nneka Carter Young, Interview

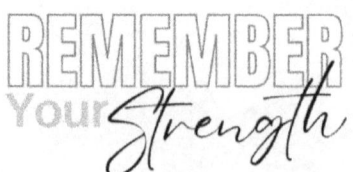

A PRODUCT OF RESILIENCE

A few months after I truly surrendered to God, on a virtual book signing I watched my friend's village rally around her and hoist her above their shoulders. On that Zoom call I had to face some hard questions from myself. I thought, "Why don't you allow yourself to be supported the way you support other people in your life?" That question added velocity to tears that were already falling from my eyes, yet the thoughts continued. "She listened to every instruction you gave her, and she sold almost 200 copies of her book within two weeks! Why don't you take your own advice?"

I was numb. "I don't know," I admitted, closing my eyes to refocus. I wiped tears and tried to look at the screen, but the disappointment that was introducing itself to me blurred my vision.

I sat with my emotions for a few seconds before taking a few deep breaths. As I listened and celebrated my friend, I opened my journal and started writing to give myself the space to hear and feel what was happening around me. As I listened to Jai answer questions beautifully about her story and her book, I turned toward what I had been running from – myself. "You're not doing enough." That thought crossed my mind and pulled my attention away from the discussion.

I wrote these questions in my journal:

- What has deepened my love?
- How has my faith been stretched?
- When has my courage been fortified?
- What does restoration feel like?

My legacy, destiny, and purpose were revealed to me through fresh eyes. I knew that it was time to ask my village to rally around me. I had isolated myself. I was in an environment that constantly caused me to question my gifts, prove my talents, and fight to display the existence of my purpose. I was tired of fighting.

Jai's book signing was the inciting incident that prompted me to take a voyage to gather my own strength. In order to remember my strength, I had to reconnect with my family history, listen to stories of resilience, and write my own definition of strength. I needed to confront fear, reconcile relationships, and dig deep into my heart to uproot many rotten things that held me back. I needed to redefine and reshape how I showed up in the world;

honoring myself with the goodness, acknowledging the not so good and letting go of the reprehensible.

A couple weeks after Jai's book release. I created an experiment and started interviewing people live on social media. I invited people to join me for live conversation and twelve people volunteered immediately. A bonus of the conversations was being able to connect with friends and loved ones during the pandemic.

For the first few interviews, I asked my guests to talk about a specific statement or phrase. It was something I heard them say that resonated with me. My sister, Joi, was my first guest. We went live on her birthday to give away several journals to women in leadership on our mom's birthday. I read a quote from my mom's journal, "Permeate in joy." Joi followed up with her declaration, "Don't let anyone blow out your candle flame."

My goal was to talk to people who wanted to talk to me. If they had a business, ministry, or product, I would help them promote it. In my introduction I said, "I want to introduce my friends to my friends so that we can all do great work in the kingdom of God."

After a few conversations, my guests started asking for graphics with their photo on them so they could promote the show to their network. I had to create something, but my amateur design skills didn't attract a lot of attention. None of that mattered to me, I was in the moment, relearning obedience to God second by second. I was going back to my early days of searching for God, answering the question, "God is. . .?"

People accused me of trying to emulate podcasts that were popular at the time, hosted by celebrities. I was slightly offended by that; I was following the instructions of the Holy Spirit. Each act of obedience was allowing me to carve my way out of a dark cave with my pen one interview at a time. I just wanted to heal.

I had become overly concerned about what people thought about me. I didn't want to do anything that I thought "they" would not approve of. I didn't want to set myself up for negative judgement, I was already feeling heavy from their rejection. In that moment, going live, I was timid, but intentional about pushing myself out of my comfort zone. There was no other choice but to stand on my firm foundation of strength.

Gathering Wisdom

When I was searching for my strength, I spent over a year talking to people I love, listening to their "bounce back stories." When I first started, I didn't have a plan or a strategy, it had been four years since I had done a live broadcast. I was timid, but intentional about pushing myself out of my comfort zone. My goal was to practice being myself on camera, nothing more. I was babbling and talking over my guests. I wanted to hear people talk about when they got knocked down by life and how they got up, but I wasn't listening to them.

Those first few episodes I was distracted by writing notes because people were pouring so much wisdom into me. You can see the progression of how I improved and how I started to show up differently on camera with each episode. I changed my hair a lot and tried new makeup. "Girl, you are cute!" I said about myself one day.

Declaration =
a statement of faith

By the time I got to chat number 25, I would talk like there were 500 people in the room even when nobody was watching. I did it for me to speak my truth and tell my story. I loved being on camera! People were telling me what their declaration was.

The discussions were often wrapped in a bounce back story about how they survived a difficult situation. I wanted to hear people talk about when they got knocked down by life and how they got up. They shared their disappointments, frustrations, strength, courage, tenacity, faith, and persistence to get back up. Around episode 20, I started to think about how these conversations could help leaders create a toolkit to bounce back. It amounted to over 100 conversations with people that I care about, and it was a personal rebranding experience.

I often gave impassioned explanations about myself, my beliefs, and my heart. In one episode, "Lessons I Learned" I said, "I am a very loving and kind woman and I hope you can see the humanity in me." I talked about guarding my heart because people didn't understand me.

The first time I cried on camera was when my friend Mekelle talked about working as a nurse during the pandemic. She talked about being essential. It hit me hard to think about her being a front-line worker. I immediately became aware of the fact that I was being watched and I turned my emotions off. My friend Nneka told me to sit in those moments and not gloss over them. Beth Ruffin talked about her book "I Belong Here" which is about self-inclusion. When she was talking, I heard in my heart, "God put me in this position, and I belong here." That was a lightbulb moment for me, and I wanted to throw something at the computer because she was talking so good. She spoke to the woman I was not allowing myself to be because I was so concerned about other people's opinions. The conversation with Beth confirmed I was shifting from rejection back to Penda Lynn James.

Uncle Marv was cheering me on in the comments like he always does, "Bout time Penn!" Other people were saying things like, "Where have you been for the past four years?"

"I'm coming back and I'm taking ya'll on this journey." Their declarations were wrapped in a bounce back story about how the person I had survived a difficult situation. I learned that I put limitations on myself and wore them like a badge of honor. My guests opened their heart, and four themes emerged as my core values: love, faith, courage, and restoration.

Those conversations helped me remember this name for God: "El Roi," which means, God sees me.

Freedom (Circa 2000)

That box was a perfect situation until I remembered my strength.

I caught a glimpse of potential, broke out of the box, and crushed it.

In hot pursuit of change
I could no longer be obscure—My Daddy said, "Be a dandelion and plant your feet."

Where I belong is where my feet are planted.
Resilience will remain with me when I stand against the wind.

CONCLUSION—I REMEMBER

On my 48th birthday, my goddaughters took me and Amaris to a hibachi grill for dinner. We met another girl who was celebrating her birthday, and we all enjoyed the antics of the chef who celebrated the birthday girls. After dinner, I had a surprise get together at a friend's house. When we walked in, I was floored by the beautiful rose-themed decorations. I toasted with a glass of ginger ale, and they had wine. "How can I be a First, lady and have a glass of wine?" I thought to myself.

After having a few snacks, playing some games, and breaking the ice, I looked at the wine bottle and something said, "Just taste it." I asked for a small glass, and within the few seconds that I took a sip, commented at how it didn't taste "too alcoholy," my phone rang. It was around 10:30 p.m. and I hadn't talked to my daddy all day. I didn't usually answer when he called late; if he had a little too much to drink, he would often tell me things my young ears didn't need to hear.

That night I answered because we hadn't talked all day. Celebrating birthdays was always a big deal in my family. I strained to hear him over the music that was playing. "Hey!" I heard him say, "Is this where the party is?" He always said that when he walked into any room.

I cackled, "Yes!"

"How you doin' baby?"

"I'm good, Daddy."

"Happy Birthday."

"Thank you, Daddy. I'm out with friends and Amaris. We went to dinner, and someone surprised me with a get together at her house."

"Oh, yeah? Tell them to give you some Mad Dog 20/20." I laughed because he claimed that his favorite college drink healed everything. I don't even think they make it anymore.

"I actually just drank some wine, Dad." I smiled. "It was pretty good."

"Good for you." I heard him take a long, deep breath. It sounded like a sigh of relief and that intrigued me. "Well, tell your friends I said hi." He paused and took a breath, "I love you."

"I love you too, Daddy. I'll call you tomorrow." The next day I went to church with my family. I worked on a film script and edited a few videos while my family took their after church naps. Around six that evening, I received a call from my nephew. I heard the panic in his voice. "Auntie. Grandpa . . . Grandpa is gone." My nephew found

Daddy in his favorite seat on the couch, resting peacefully.

My heart thumped. I was dizzy. "What!" I croaked. I ran upstairs to RJ and collapsed into his arms. The sigh of relief I heard on my birthday made sense. He was ready to go, and he had given us all instructions for our lives weeks before he passed. On my birthday, when he heard that I was having a glass of wine with friends, I believe he was happy that I had finally learned the lesson of loving people without judgment. He told me that I needed a balanced life outside of being a minister's wife and felt relieved that I had finally allowed myself to live without self-imposed boundaries.

Shake off the Shells

There is a proverb that says, "The same boiling water that softens the potato hardens the egg. It's what you're made of. Not the circumstances." A few months after my father's funeral, I asked my cousin, Michal Gaston (@heavyhustle_chefgaston) to teach me how to boil an egg. He gave specific instructions:

"Don't put the egg directly into boiling water, if you do that it will disrupt it and break up the yolk of the egg. Put the egg into cold water and then bring it up to a boil. If you want a soft-boiled egg, cook it for five minutes. If you want a hard-boiled egg, you will have to cook it for seven to ten minutes.

Then when your egg is ready, you have to cool it and you do that by shocking it. That is a chef's term that means put the egg into an ice bath for two to three minutes to stop it from cooking. Once it is cooled, you can carefully crack and pull back the layers of the shell."

I asked Michal to describe himself as the egg when he experienced having COVID-19. He said, "These last two years have been hard and a process for me being the egg. I am finally unraveling the shell. The first two years was me cooking on the inside like a butterfly. It was hot. It was a lot of mental trials and now, I feel like I am at an even round spiritually. It is time for me to shake off my shells. Shake off the past. Shake of doubt. Shake off anxiety. Shake off fear and trust the process." That statement resonated with me and confirmed that healing is a journey. I was on the right track.

Dandelion Wishes

My Daddy has left me with enough wisdom to last a lifetime, but one of the most memorable lessons is about dandelions. When I was a child welfare caseworker I called to talk to my mom after a brutal day. She wasn't home, but Daddy said, "What's going on, baby?" I was shocked, yet relieved that he recognized something was wrong. I melted into a puddle of tears, which never happened because Daddy didn't like to see or hear us cry. I gave my spiel and when I was finished, he said, "Don't be a tulip, Penn."

"What do you mean?"

He spoke slowly and emphatically, "Tulips are beautiful for two weeks and then they die. Be a dandelion, strong and resilient, hard to kill. Get people to know, like, and trust you and when they see that your heart is pure, it will be fine."

After that, I saw dandelions everywhere. They would show up in the strangest places, especially when I needed a reminder of my strength. My dad's words inspired me to go back to my childlike faith and make wishes on dandelions, breathing life into the seeds and watching the wind take them places I may never physically get to go.

As we end our time together, I hope you will stand in your strength, always. Inhale courage and exhale fear, you are right where you belong. When life hits you hard, you must remember your strength in order to rise again.

...make wishes on dandelions, breathing life into the seeds and watching the wind take them places..."

~Penda L. James

REFERENCES

Gopnik, A. (2021, December 31). "Our Year in Hell." https://www.newyorker.com/culture/2020inreview/our-year-in-hell

James, P. (2013). *Girl, Pray For Me: Moving Toward Unpluckable Faith.*

James, P. (2019) *First, Lady: Called, Confident, and Committed Woman in Leadership.*

Hannah J. (2022, October 16) Sermon, "Triggers: Entitlement" https://youtu.be/4ffVxD7OYcc?si=N4XU9RETONEN2PcN

Salo, J. (2020, December 31). 2020 Events: Yep, These Things All Happened in the Year from Hell. https://nypost.com/list/major-2020-events/

The American Heritage College Dictionary, Third Edition. (1993).

Whitehead, K. (2020, December 21) 2020: The Year From Hell. https://afro.com/2020-the-yearfromhell/

"Don't be a tulip."

~"Wonderful" Will Horton,
Penda's Daddy

ABOUT THE AUTHOR

Penda L. James found her calling in college at Wilberforce University. She obtained her Master of Education Degree from Bowling Green State University and uses her education, work experience, and faith in God to contribute to her mastery in helping people curate their stories of resilience..

Penda has always found the written word fascinating. Her father, who had majored in English, told her, "When you write down your thoughts, your reader has your full attention." Unfortunately, as a teenager, she ripped up her journals because she was ashamed of her story. The revelation from her father led her to write inspirational books on goal setting, spiritual development, and faith. Penda writes to inspire people to remember their strength.

When she is not writing, Penda enjoys spending time with her family, listening to podcasts, thrifting, crafting, and reading.

Remember Your Strength
Elna C Horton

www.ingramcontent.com/pod-product-compliance
Lightning Source LLC
LaVergne TN
LVHW040741250326
834688LV00031B/387